TAKING CARE OF
BUSINESS
STUDY GUIDE

TAKING CARE OF
BUSINESS

STUDY GUIDE

ANDY STANLEY

Multnomah® Publishers Sisters, Oregon

TAKING CARE OF BUSINESS STUDY GUIDE
published by Multnomah Publishers, Inc.

© 2005 by North Point Ministries, Inc.
International Standard Book Number: 1-59052-491-8

Unless otherwise indicated, Scripture quotations are from:
The Holy Bible, New International Version
© 1973, 1984 by International Bible Society,
used by permission of Zondervan Publishing House

Multnomah is a trademark of Multnomah Publishers, Inc.,
and is registered in the U.S. Patent and Trademark Office.
The colophon is a trademark of Multnomah Publishers, Inc.

Printed in the United States of America

For information:
MULTNOMAH PUBLISHERS, INC.
POST OFFICE BOX 1720
SISTERS, OREGON 97759

05 06 07 08 09 10 — 10 9 8 7 6 5 4 3 2 1 0

Contents

Taking Care of Business

by Andy Stanley

As Christians, we know it brings God pleasure when we turn from sin, and when we serve others, and when we study His Word and pray. But it may come as a shock to learn that God also loves it when we work. That's right…work. Sure, we know God probably likes the work of the *church*. But does He really care about ditch-digging, or cleaning…or middle management?

We tend to think of work as a necessary evil…or even as a consequence of man's sin. But God actually instituted work in the Garden of Eden. And when we work, we reflect God's image—the image in which we were created. This has huge implications in our workplace. Instead of dreading work, or avoiding it, or longing for a better job, Christians are called to a perspective on work that is nothing short of worshipful.

Work can have a huge influence on our circumstances. It can determine if we're enslaved or autonomous, wealthy or poor, fulfilled or miserable. In our minds, work can become like a god that controls our happiness. Therefore it can be tempting to try to bribe, coerce, and manipulate that god to give us what we're looking for in life. Meanwhile, we forget that God is in control of our circumstances, and that the quality and attitude of our work is meant to be a source of pleasure to Him.

As it turns out, the way we evaluate the significance of what we do at work is often completely different from the way God evaluates it. And so the only way to truly reconcile our perspective about work is to examine what God has to say about it. I'm thrilled that we'll be spending the next several weeks together studying God's perspective on work and learning how we can be about the important task of *Taking Care of Business.*

Meet the Boss

There are many common misconceptions about work. But none is more significant than the identity of our true boss. *Who* you work for determines *what* you do and *how* you do it. And there are all kinds of bosses we can serve. The boss may be a person, like the guy in the corner office; or maybe it's you. But sometimes, our real boss is an inner quest for acceptance, or a fear of failure. If we're honest, there are lots of motivations that empower us to do what we do each day. Whether we're trying to earn a salary, earn a promotion, meet a quota, or please the shareholders, we can answer to a variety of different "bosses."

But from God's perspective, your boss is not someone in the company or even on the board. And it's not a mission statement, a personal career goal, or a subversive fear either. God has called us to serve one boss above all others: Himself.

In this session, we'll get a clear picture of our true boss...once and for all. And in the process, we'll discover that the assignment is the same for all of us—whoever we are, wherever we work, and whatever we do.

DIFFERENT BOSSES, SAME JOB

Everybody works for somebody—whether you work for "the man," for food, for the perks, or for power. Even if you're self-employed, the boss you serve can be money, fame, or recognition. What are some of the "bosses" you've served throughout your working life?

How might it be different to work "as unto the Lord"? How does He compare to the other bosses you've served?

EXERCISE

VIDEO NOTES

From the video message, fill in the blanks:

1. Your work has _eternal_ implications even if it has no apparent eternal value.

2. How you _perform_ at work is as important as where you work.

3. How you perform at work is as important as how you _behave_ at work.

4. Putting your heart into your work allows God to _bless_ your work.

> " There are no menial jobs, only menial attitudes. "
> —William J. Bennett

NOTES

Col. 3.23-24

Not what you do but _how_ you do it.

DISCUSSION QUESTIONS

Take a few moments to discuss your answers to these questions with the group.

1. Do you typically put your heart into your work? Why or why not?

2. In your position at work, are you more like a master or a slave? Does that make it easier to work as unto the Lord or harder?

3. How can there be eternal value in a mundane task? Explain.

4. For the Christian in the workplace, what's the difference between good *behavior* and good *performance*? Is one more important than the other?

5. Describe how your workday would be different if you decided to put ALL your heart into your work for one day.

MILEPOSTS

■ Your work has eternal implications even if it has no apparent eternal value.

■ How you perform at work is as important as where you work.

■ How you perform at work is as important as how you behave at work.

■ Putting your heart into your work allows God to bless your work.

WHAT WILL YOU DO?

This week, pick one day in which you will approach your job as if you are working unto the Lord. What time would you get there? When would you leave? What would you be sure to say? Not say? Do? Not do?

After completing the exercise, evaluate what was the most noticeable difference about that day versus other days?

THINK ABOUT IT

Some job situations are, by definition, in contradiction to God's ways. Is the nature of your job such that you can do your work as unto the Lord with a clear conscience? If not, what would need to change?

CHANGING YOUR MIND

When our conceptions about work are inaccurate, we should renew our minds by meditating on God's perspective of work. You can begin by writing down the Scripture below and carrying God's Word with you throughout the day. There's one passage for each week.

"Whatever you do, work at it with all your heart, as working for the Lord, not for men, since you know that you will receive an inheritance from the Lord as a reward. It is the Lord Christ you are serving."

COLOSSIANS 3:23–24

LAST WEEK...
We addressed one of our most common misconceptions about work—
the fact that God is our ultimate boss. Therefore, regardless of our job,
we are to work as if we are answering to Him. What we do is often not as
important as how we did it.

Session 2

Current Economic Indicators

Why is it that the same Christian values which seem so pertinent on Sunday morning can seem so irrelevant on Monday morning? Christian principles blend perfectly with issues like morality and relationships. But try to implement them in the business world and they stick out like a sore thumb. It's just not practical. If you're too gentle, the competition can crush you. If you're too honest, your customers can abandon you. And if you're too humble, your career won't go anywhere.

Sooner or later, your Christian convictions will come into conflict with the principles that drive the business world. Whether you're expected to bend the truth, take advantage of the system, or simply cheat, it's just a matter of time. And when it happens, your response will determine the direction of your career.

In this session, we'll learn why Christians never have to compromise the principles of God to maintain the blessing of God.

THE PRESSURE'S ON

When push comes to shove and we must make a decision, we often base our actions on what's most important to us deep down. In your workplace, which one of the following is most important to you?

a. Job security

b. Recognition

c. Career progress

Explain your answer to the group.

EXERCISE

VIDEO NOTES

From the video message, fill in the blanks:

1. Ethics are like _____ .

2. Compromising your ethics:

   ■ Causes you to lose your moral _____ .

   ■ Makes you a _____ and a hypocrite.

   ■ Causes you to forfeit the opportunity of discovering what

   _____ might have done.

> " You have enemies? Good. That means you've
> stood up for something, sometime in your life. "
> —Winston Churchill

NOTES

Daniel 3:1-19

DISCUSSION QUESTIONS

Take a few moments to discuss your answers to these questions with the group.

1. Have you ever been asked to compromise your convictions at work? What emotions surfaced during that experience?

2. What are some of the pressures that can tempt us to compromise our Christian values on the job?

3. Have you ever seen someone blatantly violate Christian principles in the name of business? Were there visible consequences for that person? What was your impression of that person?

4. Which has played a greater role in your career accomplishments: your efforts or God's grace? Explain.

5. What might you lose if you always did what's right in the marketplace? What might you gain?

MILEPOSTS

■ Ethics are like water, seeping into all areas of life.

■ Compromising your ethics causes you to lose your moral authority.

■ The stories that captivate our imaginations are the ones in which God miraculously intervenes.

■ You should never compromise the principles of God to maintain the blessing of God.

WHAT WILL YOU DO?

Which of the three idols discussed in the video are you most likely to serve? In the opening exercise, you stated which factor was most likely to influence your actions at work—Job security; Recognition; or Career progress. Your answer to this question reveals which of the three idols represents the greatest threat to your convictions. In the space below, briefly describe why God is ultimately in control of this factor in your life.

THINK ABOUT IT

If God is in control of the outcomes in your career, you never have to worry about job security, recognition, or career progress again. You are free to do ANYTHING it takes to stand by your convictions. With this newfound freedom, is there any aspect of your work you'd like to approach differently from now on? Explain.

CHANGING YOUR MIND

Meditate on this verse throughout the week as a reminder that God, not your employer, ultimately controls the outcomes in your career.

"Those who honor me I will honor,
but those who despise me will be disdained."

1 SAMUEL 2:30

Session 3

The Corner Office

What qualities do you think should be required of a good employer? Take a look at the companies around you and you'll discover a wide variety of philosophies. Most agree that paying employees a competitive salary is important...and health insurance benefits can be vital too. Some employers pride themselves on providing good leadership, sharing company profits, paid vacations, and nice offices. And still others believe in giving people a chance to make something of themselves. But are all those things enough?

According to the Bible, there's more to being an employer than simply making sure your compensation package is competitive in your industry. Bosses, managers, and supervisors also have a spiritual responsibility that goes beyond company standards and industry expectations.

In this session, we'll get to the heart of how our Christian faith impacts our responsibilities as owners and leaders in the marketplace. And we'll get a picture of what it looks like when an employer incorporates Christian ethics into company policy.

WORKING MEMORIES

In the space below, list (up to) the last five jobs you've held.

_____

_____

_____

_____

_____

Beside each job listed above, indicate which of the following you MOST remember about working there:

a. How much you were paid

b. How well you were treated

EXERCISE

VIDEO NOTES

From the video message, fill in the blanks:

1. Masters are to provide what is right and

    _____.

2. Gifts from the Boss:
    ■ Uncompromising _____ :

       "I will do what is right even when it is hard."
    ■ Personal _____ :

       "You will be better off for having worked here."

4. Employees don't want to be a return on investment, they

    want to be the _____ .

5. Everybody in your company is going to

    _____ .

> " Leaders don't create followers,
> they create more leaders. "
>   —Tom Peters

NOTES

DISCUSSION QUESTIONS

Take a few moments to discuss your answers to these questions with the group.

1. In our culture, are employers typically expected to give their employees anything beyond money and benefits? Why or why not?

2. Have you ever known an owner/leader who gave more than was expected? How did that impact your perception of that person as a leader?

3. Which is the greatest responsibility for the owner/leader: company profits or employee well-being? Explain.

4. What would "right and fair" look like in your arena of work?

5. What might an owner/leader need to sacrifice in order to ensure that his employees receive what is right and fair? Is that a wise trade-off? Why or why not?

MILEPOSTS

- Masters are to provide what is right and fair.

- The owner/leader should cultivate personal development in his employees and uncompromising character in himself.

- Employees don't want to be a return on investment, they want to be the investment.

WHAT WILL YOU DO?

If you could create the ultimate employee environment, what would it look like? How would employees be compensated, encouraged, developed, inspired, supported, and affirmed? In the space below, describe some of the attributes of your ultimate workplace.

THINK ABOUT IT

God cares about salary and benefits. But an even higher priority for Him is to see us leverage our respective places in life to impact those around us for Christ. What is one way you can leverage your position in the company this week to go beyond what is required and serve someone at work in the name of Christ.

CHANGING YOUR MIND

The responsibility of the employer is not defined by a compensation package. This concept can be counterintuitive to our normal business instincts. Therefore, train your mind with this principle by meditating on this verse throughout the week.

"Do nothing out of selfish ambition or vain conceit, but in humility consider others better than yourselves. Each of you should look not only to your own interests, but also to the interests of others."

PHILIPPIANS 2:3–4

Session 4

Going Public

As we're discovering throughout this series, the requirements for a Christian in the marketplace go beyond the typical employee responsibilities. For example, a Christian worker should be someone who works as unto the Lord. He should be someone who stands on conviction. Not to mention, he should be faithful, punctual, and proficient.

But above all, Christians are to be a light to the world. As we're about to see, light is designed to shine in darkness. And for many

Christians, the workplace is the best example of a dark place where light needs to be shining.

But what exactly does it look like to be a light at work? Well, in this session we'll examine the origins of Jesus' instruction to be the light of the world. And we'll examine some practical ways you can help point your coworkers toward the light of Christ.

WHERE'D YOU GET THAT?

Some of the most helpful information in life comes as a result of interacting with coworkers. Whenever we make an exciting discovery, it's only natural to want to share the news with our friends at work or in the neighborhood. What important or helpful information have you gleaned because someone else shared it with you?

Why does the notion of sharing religious convictions or faith discoveries seem to be governed by a different set of rules?

EXERCISE

VIDEO NOTES

From the video message, fill in the blanks:

1. Christians are to be the _____ to the world.

2. Suggestions for being a light to the world:

   ■ _____ is the beginning of developing yourself as a light.

   ■ _____ is a tool for sharing light.

   ■ _____ make it easier to be a light.

   ■ _____ celebrations are awesome opportunities to shine light.

> " We don't need Christians pulling out of their jobs to witness. We need Christians who will stay in the marketplace and make their faith real. "
> —Pete Hammond

NOTES

DISCUSSION QUESTIONS

Take a few moments to discuss your answers to these questions with the group.

1. When you think about sharing your faith at work, what feelings arise?

2. How dark or light is your workplace? Explain.

3. Has anyone at work ever noticed something about your faith and asked why you're different? Why or why not?

4. What's the most compelling reason you know for sharing your faith at work?

5. What's the biggest obstacle to sharing your faith at work? How might you overcome it?

MILEPOSTS

- Christians are to be the light to the world.

- Character is the beginning of developing yourself as a light.

- Information is a tool for sharing light.

- Invitations make it easier to be a light.

- Seasonal celebrations are opportunities to shine light.

WHAT WILL YOU DO?

Sharing your faith at work is not an event, it's a process. That means you can take even the smallest step to get in the game. It may be simply noticing where your coworkers are on the spiritual continuum; or praying for opportunities to be a light; or thinking ahead about what you might say. What is one step you can take this week to be a light in the workplace?

THINK ABOUT IT

When you live out your faith in every aspect of life, it becomes an integral part of every routine interaction you have with people. Including those at work. Does Christ tend to be such a focal point in your life that He comes up in everyday conversation? Why or why not?

CHANGING YOUR MIND

Meditate on this verse to remind you of your primary calling in the workplace.

"You are the light of the world. A city on a hill cannot be hidden."

MATTHEW 5:14

Session 5

Paying Your Dues

Working as unto the Lord can be one of the most exhilarating and fulfilling experiences you will ever know. There's nothing like coming to work knowing that you are applying your skills and talents to do the best job you can do...and that the excellence you achieve is glorifying your Father in heaven.

But what happens when the people over you prevent you from doing the job to the level of your potential? What happens when they fail to see your potential, or understand your vision, or give you the latitude you need to excel? What happens when they don't have the wisdom you possess and their decisions actually undermine what could have been great progress for the company, and great success for you?

It's not unusual to find yourself in a situation where your boss simply isn't as smart as you are. And suddenly, it seems as though your ability to work as unto the Lord is hindered by someone who may not understand or embrace the Christian values you strive to serve. What should you do then?

In this session, we'll look at who's really behind the people who call the shots in your workplace. The answer may surprise you. If we don't know how to respond to those who are in authority over us, we could actually thwart or destroy what God is trying to accomplish in our workplace.

That Depends on Who

In which of the following situations are you MOST likely to require additional information before giving your commitment? Rank them in order.

a. The president of the United States invites you to attend a seminar

b. Your pastor invites you to attend a seminar

c. Your spouse invites you to attend a seminar

EXERCISE

d. Your boss invites you to attend a seminar

e. Your insurance agent invites you to attend a seminar

If you had to name the one factor that determines how you prioritize these scenarios, what would it be?

VIDEO NOTES

From the video message, fill in the blanks:

1. When we don't agree with our boss, God wants us to quit looking at the *what* and look at the _____ .

2. God establishes and works _____ authorities.

3. When you fight against authority established by God, you will reap _____ .

> " The highest duty is to respect authority. "
> —Leo XIII

NOTES

DISCUSSION QUESTIONS

Take a few moments to discuss your answers to these questions with the group.

1. Has your boss ever been just plain wrong? Describe.

2. What's the hardest part about supporting the boss when he's wrong?

3. At what point should you support the boss anyway?

4. Can supporting an imperfect boss help bring about God's perfect will? Why or why not?

5. On a scale of 1–10, how good are you at supporting authorities even when they're *wrong*?

MILEPOSTS

■ When we don't agree with our boss, God wants us to quit looking at the *what* and look at the *who*.

■ God establishes all authority.

■ God works through authorities, whether they're good or bad, right or wrong.

■ When you fight against authority established by God, you will reap judgment.

WHAT WILL YOU DO?

Describe a situation at work in which you don't necessarily agree with those in authority over you. If there are none, describe a hypothetical situation.

THINK ABOUT IT

Using your imagination, describe in detail how God might be using your boss's mistakes to bring about His perfect will for your life—what might He be up to? Be creative.

CHANGING YOUR MIND

Meditate on this passage to help you remember that God always works through our authorities to bring about His perfect will.

"Everyone must submit himself to the governing authorities,
for there is no authority except that which God has established.
The authorities that exist have been established by God."

ROMANS 13:1

Session 6

Leaving Early

In your life, you are called to accomplish many things. In addition to reaching your career potential, you may have a spouse to honor and cherish, a family to raise, and a ministry to serve. To do your absolute best at any one of those endeavors would require an enormous amount of time. But there are only twenty-four hours in a day. There's just not enough time in your day to reach your full potential in every arena. In order to excel in one area, something must be neglected somewhere else.

As a result, we learn to cheat. In order to meet the demands in one area, we have to cheat someone or something in another area. We all do it.

So when it comes to work, where do you cheat? Where *should* you cheat? In this session, we'll discover that God's greatest desire is not to see you reach your full potential in every area of life...not even work. Instead, we should learn to protect our highest God-given priorities...and learn to cheat the rest.

I'M ALL ABOUT THAT

Do not read ahead. In the space below, list your top five accomplishments for the past year or two. This could be an achievement that is publicly recognized, or one that is personally satisfying. They need not be listed in any particular order.

1.

2.

3.

4.

5.

E X E R C I S E

If you have not listed your top five accomplishments yet, do not read this. After you have listed your accomplishments, place each one in a category by writing one of the following letters beside it: a. Career; b. Family/Relational; c. Finances; d. Physical/Recreational; e. Spiritual. So what are *you* all about? Where have most of your accomplishments been realized?

E X E R C I S E

VIDEO NOTES

From the video message, fill in the blanks:

1. Every single day of our lives, we _____ somebody.
2. Cheating our family communicates, "Someone else is more _____ than you are."
3. Eventually, our mental _____ is overcome by our physical weakness.
4. When the rock drops, everyone asks, "What _____ ?"

> " *You have a lifetime to work, but children are only young once.* "
> —*Polish Proverb*

NOTES

DISCUSSION QUESTIONS

Take a few moments to discuss your answers to these questions with the group.

1. Where are you cheating? Who *feels* cheated?

2. Did your parent(s) give something to people at work that belonged to you?

3. Have you ever seen the rock drop? Describe.

4. Have you ever prayed that God would fill the gaps at home while you work overtime?

5. What would be the consequences if you cheat at work? At home?

MILEPOSTS

■ There's not enough time in the day to get everything done.

■ Every single day of our lives, we cheat somebody or something.

■ Cheating your family communicates, "Someone else is more important than you are."

WHAT WILL YOU DO?

The time to decide where you will cheat is before you know the outcome and the consequences. You must resolve in your heart to honor your top priorities regardless. And that means cheating everything else. So where will you draw the lines for your work? Is it a certain time by which you'll be home every day? Is it a limit for travel days? In the space below and on the next page, declare the parameters that are nonnegotiable for your family. Then try a thirty-day test. After thirty days, evaluate how you are doing at honoring your top priorities.

THINK ABOUT IT

God often intervenes to provide and protect when we obey our calling at home and trust Him with the outcome. What strategy can you implement this week to begin trusting God with your work and applying your loyalty at home where it belongs most?

CHANGING YOUR MIND

Meditating on Scripture is the best way to align your desires with God's desires for you. Carry this passage of Scripture with you this week as a reminder of your primary need in life.

"'Martha, Martha,' the Lord answered, 'you are worried
and upset about many things, but only one thing is needed.
Mary has chosen what is better, and it will not be taken away from her.'"

LUKE 10:41–42

LEADER'S GUIDE

So, You're the Leader...

Is that intimidating? Perhaps exciting? No doubt you have some mental pictures of what it will look like, what you will say, and how it will go. Before you get too far into the planning process, there are some things you should know about leading a small-group discussion. We've compiled some tried and true techniques here to help you.

BASICS ABOUT LEADING

1. **Don't teach...facilitate**—Perhaps you've been in a Sunday school class or Bible study in which the leader could answer any question and always had something interesting to say. It's easy to think you need to be like that too. Relax. You don't. Leading a small group is quite different. Instead of being the featured act at the party, think of yourself as the host or hostess behind the scenes. Your primary job is to create an environment where people feel comfortable and to keep the meeting generally on track. Your party is most successful when your guests do most of the talking.

2. **Cultivate discussion**—It's also easy to think that the meeting lives or dies by *your* ideas. In reality, what makes a small-group meeting successful are the ideas of everyone in the group. The most valuable thing you can do is to get people to share their thoughts. That's how the relationships in your group will grow and thrive. Here's a rule: The impact of your study material will typically never exceed the impact of the relationships through which it was studied. The more meaningful the relationships, the more meaningful the study. In a sterile environment, even the best material is suppressed.

3. **Point to the material**—A good host or hostess gets the party going by offering delectable hors d'oeuvres and beverages. You too should be ready to serve up "delicacies" from the material. Sometimes you will simply read the discussion questions and invite everyone to respond. At other times, you may encourage someone to share their own ideas. Remember, some of the best treats are the ones your guests will bring to the party. Go with the flow of the meeting, and be ready to pop out of the kitchen as needed.

4. **Depart from the material**—A talented ministry team has carefully designed this study for your small group. But

that doesn't mean you should follow every part word for word. Knowing how and when to depart from the material is a valuable art. Nobody knows more about your people than you do. The narratives, questions, and exercises are here to provide a framework for discovery. However, every group is motivated differently. Sometimes, the best way to start a small-group discussion is simply to ask, "Does anyone have any personal insights or revelations they'd like to share from this week's material?" Then sit back and listen.

5. **Stay on track**—Conversation is like the currency of a small-group discussion. The more interchange, the healthier the "economy." However, you need to keep your objectives in mind. If your goal is to have a meaningful experience with this material, then you should make sure the discussion is contributing to that end. It's easy to get off on a tangent. Be prepared to interject politely and refocus the group. You may need to say something like, "Excuse me, we're obviously all interested in this subject; however, I just want to make sure we cover all the material for this week."

6. **Above all, pray**—The best communicators are the ones who manage to get out of God's way enough to let Him

communicate *through* them. That's important to keep in mind. Books don't teach God's Word; neither do sermons or group discussions. God Himself speaks into the hearts of men and women, and prayer is our vital channel to communicate directly with Him. Cover your efforts in prayer. You don't just want God present at your meeting, you want Him to direct it.

We hope you find these suggestions helpful. And we hope you enjoy leading this study. You will find additional guides and suggestions for each session in the Leader's Guide notes that follow.

Leader's Guide
Session Notes

SESSION 1—MEET THE BOSS

KEY POINT

There are a lot of different motivations for working. But the main point of this session is that, according to the Bible, we should do our work as if God is our boss. This principle is an important foundation for the rest of this study. When we work as unto the Lord, it instantly realigns many priorities and brings our ambitions in subjection to God's will.

EXERCISE—DIFFERENT BOSSES, SAME JOB

This exercise is designed to get participants thinking about some of the motivations—or "bosses"—behind our ambitions for working. What you serve at work—whether a person, a value, or an ambition—determines your actions and attitudes. When we choose to serve God, it has a direct impact on the spirit of our work.

VIDEO NOTES

1. Your work has <u>eternal</u> implications even if it has no apparent eternal value.
2. How you <u>perform</u> at work is as important as where you work.
3. How you perform at work is as important as how you <u>behave</u> at work.
4. Putting your heart into your work allows God to <u>bless</u> your work.

NOTES FOR DISCUSSION QUESTIONS:

1. Do you typically put your heart into your work? Why or why not?

   The purpose of this question is to begin a process of self-assessment. Since this may be the first chance for participants to open up and share, be honest and transparent, so as to encourage participation from everyone. Create an environment in which it's okay to admit that motives aren't always pure. The more we are open and honest, the more participants will be encouraged to take an honest look at themselves. This begins with the leader.

2. In your position at work, are you more like a master or a slave? Does that make it easier to work as unto the Lord or harder?

This is another important observation to make about our workplace. Participants should assess the dynamics that are in place for them personally. This question also suggests that we have similarities to the apostle Paul's audience in the Bible passage for this session.

3. How can there be eternal value in a mundane task? Explain.

This question refers participants to the point in the video message about our responsibility to be good stewards of our opportunities. Our performance impacts our eternal destiny. Encourage the people in your group to think about this concept thoroughly.

4. For the Christian in the workplace, what's the difference between good *behavior* and good *performance?*

   As pointed out in the video, good behavior is adherence to moral, ethical, and etiquette guidelines. Good performance is excellence in the execution of your job function. It is possible to have excellent "Christian" behavior while doing a lousy job. Christians should strive for excellence in both arenas.

5. Describe how your workday would be different if you decided to put ALL your heart into your work for one day.

   The purpose of this question is to prompt participants to begin envisioning how to work as unto the Lord in their own jobs. What would it look like? What would it take? Where would you begin?

WHAT WILL YOU DO?

Participants are to pick one day and conduct this trial. Discuss your experiences together. With one day under your belt, the path is paved for ongoing change. Remember, God is ultimately responsible for working change in our hearts. Often, His work is not instantaneous, but more long-term and permanent in nature. Don't be discouraged because it doesn't come easily.

THINK ABOUT IT

A portion of the population works in situations that inherently require them to participate in unethical or even immoral activities. This may require a change of job descriptions or even a change of jobs. God will honor the resolve of everyone who accepts the call to pursue work that is pleasing to Him.

SESSION 2—CURRENT ECONOMIC INDICATORS

KEY POINT

God is in control of our circumstances, even at work. God can give you a raise or a promotion. He can make you successful in the most unexpected of ways. Because of this fact, it's safe for you to follow His principles even when they seem to go against the grain of what is normal or expected at work. You should stand strong on your convictions even when it's inconvenient, awkward, or appears to cost you personally.

EXERCISE—THE PRESSURE'S ON

When the pressure's on, our decisions tend to default back to what's most important to us. Your answers to this exercise will make more sense after viewing the video message for this session. In the meantime, this will get participants thinking about what drives them most while on the job.

VIDEO NOTES

1. Ethics are like <u>water</u>.

2. Compromising your ethics:

   ■ Causes you to lose your moral <u>authority</u>.

   ■ Makes you a <u>coward</u> and a hypocrite.

   ■ Causes you to forfeit the opportunity of discovering what <u>God</u> might have done.

NOTES FOR DISCUSSION QUESTIONS

1. Have you ever been asked to compromise your convictions at work? What emotions surfaced during that experience?

   The purpose of this question is to generate conversation and to get participants to evaluate the environment they work in. Does it encourage their Christian convictions or erode them? And equally important, what natural reaction does that evoke?

2. What are some of the pressures that can tempt us to compromise our Christian values on the job?

   Before we can learn to stand on our convictions, it's helpful to examine what forces are pulling us in the opposite direction. Is it the desire for acceptance? Is it fear of rejection? Greed? When we can identify our inner conflicts, it becomes easier to choose the best path.

3. Have you ever seen someone blatantly violate Christian principles in the name of business? Were there visible consequences for that person? What was your impression of that person?

   Whenever someone violates Christian principles in the marketplace, there will be a consequence somewhere. This question is an invitation to observe how this principle plays out in the real world. However, it is important to note that the effects are not always immediate. We must trust that God will be faithful to honor those who are faithful in the end.

4. Which has played a greater role in your career accomplishments: your efforts or God's grace? Explain.

It is important to realize that although our hard work can maximize our opportunities, only God's grace allows us to accomplish career milestones. God alone equips us with the skills, talents, and the opportunity to work, as well as protects us from factors that would create setbacks.

5. What might you lose if you always did what's right in the marketplace? What might you gain?

It's important to count the cost of doing what's right. In the end, we must choose to trust that God will show Himself strong on our behalf when we are faithful to honor His ways in the marketplace. However, it is important to note that the effects are not always immediate.

WHAT WILL YOU DO?

This question builds on the opening exercise that reveals which of the three idols from the video message a person is likely to serve. Now participants should write out the truth about God's ultimate control over their circumstances. They should be encouraged to trust God and act on faith instead of human business logic.

THINK ABOUT IT

Here you are trying to encourage participants to identify specific steps of faith they can take as a result of the principles learned this week. Each person should try to name one or two situations in which they can entrust their situation to God.

SESSION 3—THE CORNER OFFICE

KEY POINT

The responsibility of the employer/supervisor goes beyond the mere business transactions of employment. A boss/leader should also be interested in the well-being of each person and cultivate an environment that encourages each one's personal development. The workplace is simply one more arena in a temporary life in which we have the opportunity to share what is eternal—God's love.

EXERCISE—WORKING MEMORIES

Typically, people are much more likely to recall how they were treated at a job than how much they were paid. As an employer, your legacy rests more in how much you value a person than in how much you pay a person.

VIDEO NOTES

1. Masters are to provide what is right and <u>fair</u>.
2. Gifts from the Boss:
   - Uncompromising <u>Character</u>: "I will do what is right even when it is hard."
   - Personal <u>Development</u>: "You will be better off for having worked here."
4. Employees don't want to be a return on investment, they want to be the <u>investment</u>.
5. Everybody in your company is going to <u>leave</u>.

NOTES FOR DISCUSSION QUESTIONS:

1. In our culture, are employers typically expected to give their employees anything beyond money and benefits? Why or why not?

   No, they are not. Our culture generally propagates a secular business ethic, not a Christian ethic. For the Christian, there is no area of life that is not sacred. Therefore, Christians are to give employees what is right and fair, not just a monetary arrangement.

2. Have you ever known an owner/leader who gave more than was expected? How did that impact your perception of that person as a leader?

   The impact of a generous, caring leader is usually significantly more positive than the average.

3. Which is the greatest responsibility for the owner/leader: company profits or employee well-being? Explain.

   This question reiterates the main point of the session: that Christian bosses/owners should not strive for profits at the expense of the way they nurture their employees.

4. What would "right and fair" look like in your arena of work?

   Encourage each participant to consider some appropriate action steps for their particular situation.

5. What might an owner/leader need to sacrifice in order to ensure that his employees receive what is right and fair?

   As this question suggests, we must be willing to make sacrifices on the way to expressing the way we value our employees. It's okay to accept lower profitability if it enables you to nurture people better.

Is that a wise trade-off? Why or why not?

It can be a wise trade-off, because the fruit of applying
Christian principles to our business relationships is eternal fruit, whereas the value of earthly profit is short-lived
by comparison.

WHAT WILL YOU DO?

This is an opportunity to dream and think outside the box. If you could
start from scratch, what would you create? This exercise allows participants to apply the concepts of this session without limitations.

THINK ABOUT IT

This question gives people the chance to think ahead about some specific ways in which they could serve and reach others for Christ in their
work environment.

SESSION 4—GOING PUBLIC

KEY POINT

Christians are to be many things in the workplace, but above all, they are to be lights to the world. This session examines what that looks like in the business arena and puts forward several specific ways to point others toward the light of Christ.

EXERCISE—WHERE'D YOU GET THAT?

Sharing your faith at work is as natural as sharing anything else that interests you or excites you. But, as this exercise suggests, we sometimes operate by a different set of rules when it comes to spiritual matters. But that need not limit us. We should still pursue opportunities to share the life-changing message of Christ with others.

VIDEO NOTES

1. Christians are to be the <u>light</u> to the world.

2. Suggestions for being a light to the world:
   - <u>Character</u> is the beginning of developing yourself as a light.
   - <u>Information</u> is a tool for sharing light.
   - <u>Invitations</u> make it easier to be a light.
   - <u>Seasonal</u> celebrations are awesome opportunities to shine light.

NOTES FOR DISCUSSION QUESTIONS:

1. When you think about sharing your faith at work, what feelings arise?
   The purpose of this question is to cultivate introspection. Your feelings about sharing your faith tell you where you are in the process of embracing this responsibility. They also suggest how you can begin to move toward a lifestyle of sharing your faith at work.

2. How dark or light is your workplace? Explain.

   Another logical step to take is to assess the receptivity of your workplace, as this question suggests.

3. Has anyone at work ever noticed something about your faith and asked why you're different? Why or why not?

   The main purpose of this question is to prompt participants to consider what it might look like to live out their faith in a way that is noticeable. If they've ever been noticed at work before, they can analyze what worked about it so they may develop it further. If not, they can consider how to take steps toward developing character that stands out.

4. What's the most compelling reason you know for sharing your faith at work?

   There are many answers to this question. The main purpose is to get participants to focus on the important reasons for being a light to the world.

5. What's the biggest obstacle to sharing your faith at work? How might you overcome it?

Obstacles are the only things that stand between us and the goal of sharing our faith. An obstacle well-defined is an obstacle half-resolved.

What Will You Do?

This assignment will push participants toward action by thinking proactively. Taking a step, even if it's not the perfect one yet, helps people begin to improve at sharing their faith.

Think About It

Perhaps the most important foundation for sharing your faith is a vibrant, personal relationship with God. When your relationship with Him is active and real, the evidence overflows naturally in a way that is visible to others.

SESSION 5—PAYING YOUR DUES

KEY POINT

Submission to our authorities at work is crucial, even when our authorities are not as wise as we are (or think we are). As long as we are not being asked to violate God's rules for morality or ethics, we can confidently obey orders and trust God with the outcome.

EXERCISE—THAT DEPENDS ON WHO

This exercise points out that many of our attitudes and decisions are based on who is involved. There is nothing wrong with this. In fact, as this session suggests, we should react to instructions and requests at work based on who issues them, not so much on what is being asked of us.

VIDEO NOTES

1. When we don't agree with our boss, God wants us to quit looking at the *what* and look at the *who*.
2. God establishes and works through authorities.
3. When you fight against authority established by God, you will reap judgment.

NOTES FOR DISCUSSION QUESTIONS:

1. Has your boss ever been just plain wrong? Describe.

   The main purpose of this question is to generate conversation about authorities at work. As discussion will likely
   reveal, it is common to see owners/supervisors make
   mistakes. The important thing is that we know how to
   respond when it happens.

2. What's the hardest part about supporting the boss when
   he's wrong?

   When the boss is wrong, it introduces a tension between
   our need to be submissive and our desire to help the
   company avoid a setback. The point of this session is
   that once we've fulfilled our responsibility of sharing our
   opinion, we can focus on the singular assignment of fulfilling the boss's requests.

3. At what point should you support the boss anyway?

   You should support the boss once you have made a rea-
   sonable attempt to share your objections, or once he or
   she has made it clear that they do not desire your input
   at this point. Your objections should only be presented

for the purpose of helping your boss succeed, not to serve your own interests.

4. Can supporting an imperfect boss help bring about God's perfect will? Why or why not?

Yes, it can. God works through all circumstances to bring about His will. While God does not initiate unwise actions or cause bad things to happen, He is able to work them together for good. If we respond to wrong by rejecting authority, that only makes matters worse.

5. On a scale of 1–10, how good are you at supporting authority even when they're *wrong?*

The purpose of this question is to provide a helpful self-analysis. Simply stopping to think about our attitudes toward authority can be enlightening.

What Will You Do?

The purpose of this exercise is to identify specific areas for personal application of this session's message. If there are no known problematic situations, participants may discover the areas most likely to become a problem in the future.

Think About It

It can be very helpful and encouraging to consider the ways God might use our unpleasant experiences for good. This exercise may not reveal the exact purposes of God, but it will bolster participants' confidence in God's sovereignty in every situation.

SESSION 6—LEAVING EARLY

KEY POINT

There's not enough time in the day to get everything done to perfection. As a result, we make subconscious decisions every day to "cheat" one area in order to take care of another. The point of this session is that we should be careful not to cheat at home for the sake of work. Instead, we should cheat work in order to take care of things at home.

EXERCISE—I'M ALL ABOUT THAT

This exercise will reveal where participants have NOT been cheating. From there, it should be easy to speculate possible areas of neglect. Often, participants discover a tendency to achieve at work while overlooking responsibilities at home.

VIDEO NOTES

1. Every single day of our lives, we <u>cheat</u> somebody.
2. Cheating our family communicates, "Someone else is more <u>important</u> than you are."

3. Eventually, our mental <u>willingness</u> is overcome by our physical weakness.

4. When the rock drops, everyone asks, "What <u>happened</u>?"

Notes for Discussion Questions:

1. Where are you cheating? Who *feels* cheated?
   The purpose of this question is to prompt participants to consider whether they are cheating something important to them for the sake of work. This can be an eye-opening moment.

2. Did your parent(s) give something to people at work that belonged to you?
   Often, we get our attitudes and behaviors about work and home from our parents' example. This question will give participants a chance to consider whether the example they grew up with is the best one. It will also enable them to appreciate what it feels like when a parent chooses to serve work over home. Although the parent's intentions may be good, children and spouses

rarely feel more loved as the result of excessive focus on work.

3. Have you ever seen the rock drop? Describe.

Once they think about it, many participants may realize that they've seen the impact of overwork on the family.

4. Have you ever prayed that God would fill the gaps at home while you work overtime?

Some participants may realize that they have followed a common misconception that it is acceptable to neglect our calling at home so as to pursue greater advances at work. As was suggested in this session, that should not be our approach.

5. What would be the consequences if you cheat at work? At home?

The purpose of this question is to prompt participants to weigh the costs in each arena. When you look at it in those terms, it is easier to prioritize home over work.

WHAT WILL YOU DO?

This exercise will prompt participants to identify specific boundaries to set at work in order to protect home life.

THINK ABOUT IT

Part of developing a strategy for work is to anticipate the times when you must rely on God to intervene on your behalf. God has given us a hands-on responsibility at home; we must take action there while entrusting work and career to Him.

Life Rules
Instructions for the Game of Life

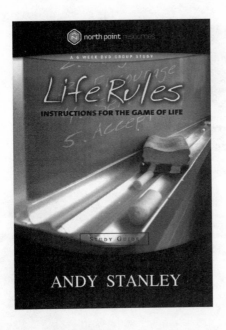

God's guidelines for living are for your
protection and freedom. Learn them, live by
them, and experience the dramatic, positive
change in every area of your life.

Study Guide 1-59052-493-4
DVD 1-59052-494-2

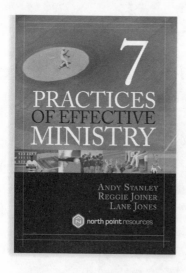

7 PRACTICES OF EFFECTIVE MINISTRY

Andy Stanley, Lane Jones, Reggie Joiner

An insightful and entertaining parable for every ministry leader who yearns for a more simplified approach to ministry.

ISBN: 1-59052-373-3
$19.99 Hardback
Church Resources

CREATING COMMUNITY

Andy Stanley and Bill Willits

Creating Community delivers a successful template for building and nurturing small groups in your church. Andy Stanley and Bill Willits reveal the formula developed over ten years at North Point Community Church for one of the most successful and admired small group ministries in the country.

ISBN: 1-59052-396-2
$19.99 Hardback
Church Resources

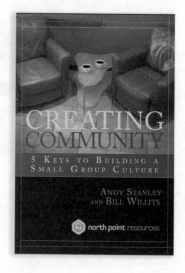

DISCOVERING GOD'S WILL STUDY GUIDE & DVD
Andy Stanley

God has a personal vision for your life and He wants you to know it even more than you do. Determining God's will can be a difficult process, especially when we need to make a decision in a hurry. In this eight part series, Andy Stanley discusses God's providential, moral, and personal will and how He uses other people and the principles of Scripture to guide us.

STUDY GUIDE 1-59052-379-2, $9.99
DVD 1-59052-380-6, $24.99

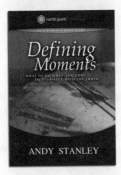

PARENTAL GUIDANCE STUDY GUIDE & DVD
Andy Stanley and Reggie Joiner

Our lives are influenced by our relationships, experiences, and decisions. Therefore our priority as parents should be to enhance our child's relationship with us, advance our child's relationship with God, and influence our child's relationship with those outside the home.

STUDY GUIDE 1-59052-381-4, $9.99
DVD 1-59052-378-4, $24.99

DEFINING MOMENTS STUDY GUIDE & DVD
Andy Stanley

It is no secret that what you don't know CAN hurt you. In spite of that, we still go out of our way at times to avoid the truth. Learn how to discern the truth and apply those "defining moments" in your life with this DVD and study guide.

STUDY GUIDE 1-59052-464-0, $9.99
DVD 1-59052-465-9, $24.99

THE BEST QUESTION EVER STUDY GUIDE & DVD
Andy Stanley

Can you think of a question that has the potential to foolproof your relationships, your marriage, your finances, even your health? A question that, had you asked it and followed its leading, would have enabled you to avoid your greatest regret? Read *The Best Question Ever Study Guide* to find out how to foolproof your life.

STUDY GUIDE 1-59052-462-4, $9.99
DVD 1-59052-463-2, $24.99